Newport Community Learning & Libraries
Cymuned ddysgu a Llyfrgelloedd Casnewydd

THIS ITEM SHOULD BE RETURNED OR
RENEWED BY THE LAST DATE
STAMPED BELOW

Newport
CITY COUNCIL
CYNGOR DINAS
Casnewydd

Bettws Library & Information Centre

0 7 JUN 2012   Tel: 656656

J

2 8 MAR 2013

1 7 MAY 2013

**To renew telephone 656656 or 656657 (minicom)
or www.newport.gov.uk/libraries**

ADRENALIN RUSH

MOUNTAIN BIKING

ANNE-MARIE LAVAL

W

FRANKLIN WATTS
LONDON • SYDNEY

First published in 2011 by
Franklin Watts
338 Euston Road
London NW1 3BH

Franklin Watts Australia
Level 17/207 Kent Street
Sydney NSW 2000

Produced by Tall Tree Ltd

A CIP catalogue record for this book is available
from the British Library.

Dewey Classification 796.6'3

ISBN: 978 1 4451 0476 8

Printed in China

Franklin Watts is a division of Hachette Children's
Books, an Hachette UK company.

www.hachette.co.uk

Disclaimer
The website addresses (URLs) included in this
book were valid at the time of going to press.
However, because of the nature of the Internet, it
is possible that some addresses have changed, or
sites may have changed or closed down since
publication. While the author and publisher regret
any inconvenience this may cause to readers, no
responsibility for any such changes can be
accepted either by the author or the publisher.

In preparation of this book, all due care has been
exercised with regard to the advice, activities and
techniques depicted. The publishers regret that
they can accept no liability for any loss or injury
sustained. When learning a new activity, it is
important to get expert tuition and to follow a
manufacturer's instructions.

Words in **bold** are in the glossary on page 30.

CONTENTS

'Hit the dirt' is a mountain biking (MTB) phrase. It is the kind of thing you might say to your friend as you are about to start a ride together: 'Let's hit the dirt.' It also has another meaning – crashing!

This mountain bike racer is taking part in an event in hills above the sea in the Western Cape, South Africa.

The most popular bike

What is it that makes MTB so popular? Partly it is because many people think the bikes look really cool. But mostly it is because it is just so much fun. With the right mountain bike you can:

• race your mates down narrow trails through the woods.

• go **dirt jumping**.

• enter a cyclo-cross race.

• ride down a World Cup downhill course.

• go away for a weekend camping in the wilderness.

• ride to school, the shops or a friend's house.

Mountain bikes really can do everything that can be done on two wheels.

World of mountain bikes

Turn up to any **trailhead** in the world, and you will probably find mountain bikers getting ready to ride. Usually you get a warm welcome, especially if you give people a smile and a hello. MTB is a friendly sport, and most mountain bikers will help each other out with advice on where to ride, or help repair a puncture or a mechanical problem.

MTB features cross-country races (above), long-distance events with overnight camping (left) and much more.

Three top MTB videos

MTB videos are often published in series; you can find clips of them on YouTube. Here are three of the best:
- *Earthed – some of the most extreme downhill, ridden by some of the best riders in the world.*
- *New World Disorder – focuses on **freeride MTB**, but there is lots of dirt jumping and street riding, too.*
- *Kranked – this series contains all kinds of riding, but Kranked 6: Progression features some amazing North Shore trails.*

People have been riding off-road for many years. It is only fairly recently, though, that bikes built especially for off-road riding were developed.

Special CX bikes have drop handlebars, like road bikes. You can enter most 'cross' races on a mountain bike, too.

Cyclo-cross

Some people say that the earliest form of MTB is cyclo-cross (CX) racing, which started in the early 1900s. In a CX race, riders start at the same time, and follow a pre-set course. They ride as hard as they can for an hour, then finish the lap on which they are riding. The rider who has completed the most laps, wins.

The Breezer series II was one of the first ever purpose-built mountain bikes.

Cruiser racers

In the 1970s, a group of Californians started driving to the top of Mount Tamalpais in Marin County, and racing back down on their old **beach cruisers**. They kept breaking their bikes, so they started building better ones. That was the start of the modern mountain-bike business. Pretty soon, children everywhere were asking for Specialized Stumpjumpers or Marin Muirwood bikes.

Joe Breeze went to school at the foot of Mount Tamalpais in California, USA, and was one of a group of friends who first started racing down its trails. Breeze built the first purpose-built mountain bike, the Breezer Series I in 1977. Only nine were made, but Breeze carried on building bikes. Today Breezer Bikes is still going strong.

Cross-country races, such as this one, are a great test of your endurance and riding skills, but they appeal only to a small number of riders.

In the 1990s, there was a massive MTB craze. People loved the idea of a bicycle that could be ridden wherever you wanted. They also liked the healthy lifestyle of cycling to the countryside, then riding along traffic-free routes. But this popularity soon caused problems.

Decline and fall

Almost as quickly as it started, the MTB craze nearly died out. There were three big reasons for this:

• the rise of the BSO – BSO is short for 'Bike-Shaped Object', a bike that looks like a mountain bike, but is cheaper than other MTBs and is not tough enough to be ridden hard. Anyone who bought one was quickly put off MTB.

• competitions became focused on circuit races, similar to CX courses. Most people find this kind of riding boring to watch and to take part in.

• access to trails began to be restricted after complaints about out-of-control mountain bikers.

The rebirth of MTB

In the early 2000s, mountain bikes became stronger, lighter and more reliable. Manufacturers developed full-suspension machines that you could ride over almost any ground. Riders began to find new things to do on their bikes rather than just riding around in circles. With better bikes and an increase in the range of things you could do on a bike, MTB once again became popular.

All mountain bikers quickly learn how to fix a puncture. Even with off-road tyres, punctures happen pretty often.

Some trails are closed to bikes because they are just for walkers or to stop soil erosion.

TRAIL CLOSED

NO BIKES ALLOWED

Trail rules
Riders developed this set of rules in the 1990s so that all trail users could live together in peace and harmony:
* *ride only where it is allowed.*
* *leave no trace – no litter and no skid marks on fresh grass.*
* *control your bike.*
* *give way to other trail users – never expect others to step aside for you.*
* *never scare animals.*

HELPFUL HINTS

Today there are many different types of mountain bike, but the best bike for all-round use is still a hard-tail. This is a machine with suspension forks at the front, but a rigid frame at the back. Hard-tail bikes combine comfort and stiffness, and can be used for just about any kind of riding.

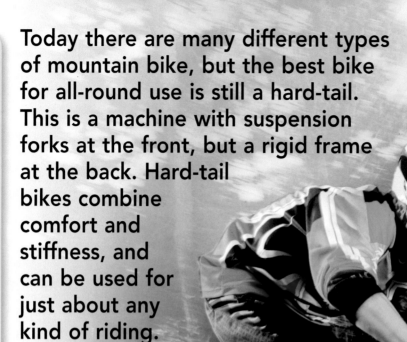

Gears
Bikes usually have 27 or 30 gears – enough to get you up or down just about any slope.

Forks
These move up and down to absorb shocks as the bike travels over rough or bumpy ground.

Tyres
Knobbly tyres give grip and a bit of shock absorption.

Clippy pedals
Many riders prefer pedals that clip to the bottom of their shoes. These make controlling the bike easier.

Full-suspension bikes have to be ridden in a slightly different style from a hard-tail. You have to keep your weight on the saddle for the rear suspension to work properly.

Disc brakes
These are the same type of brakes as are used on cars and motorbikes, so they stop lightweight bikes extremely well.

A modern hard-tail bike, such as this one, can be used for almost any kind of riding, from downhill courses to cross-country, and even off-road touring.

Bike weight varies from about 9 kg for a cross-country bike to 19 kg for a downhill bike.

Suspension usually has about 100 mm **travel** on cross-country bikes, and up to 300 mm of travel on downhill bikes.

The size of the brake discs varies from 160 mm for cross-country to 200 mm in downhill. Bigger discs give the brakes better stopping power.

Full-suspension bikes

Some riders pick full-suspension bikes with shock absorbers on the front and rear. The tyres rarely leave contact with the ground, so these bikes are fast and smooth to pedal. The suspension travel soaks up bumps, allowing riders to go more quickly over rough ground, especially downhill.

The disadvantages of full-suspension bikes are that they are usually heavier than hard-tails, and there are more moving parts that can go wrong.

Aside from a bike, you do not need a lot of equipment for MTB. The most important bit of gear is the one that protects you from serious damage – your helmet. Other pieces of equipment and clothing can make MTB life more comfortable.

Helmet
To work properly, this must be a good fit and done up tightly enough to stay on your head in an accident.

Padded shorts
These make riding for a long time more comfortable as they stop the saddle rubbing against your skin. There are two main kinds: tight lycra ones, and baggy ones with a pad inside.

Glasses
These stop dirt from the wheels being flicked up into your eyes.

Padded gloves
Long distances or hard, bouncy downhill rides will be far less punishing on your hands with a good pair of padded gloves.

MTB shoes
The stiff soles transfer power to the cranks well, and grip on the soles helps if you have to put your foot down.

Other equipment

Most mountain bikers like to carry water in a hydration pack (a backpack with a special container for water). A tube leads over the rider's shoulder, making it possible to drink with both hands on the handlebars – very handy if you are going over bumpy ground!

Many hydration packs have a bit of space for extra bits of kit. Look inside a mountain biker's hydration pack, and you would probably find:

• a pump, spare inner tube and repair patches, in case you get a puncture.

• extra bits of clothing, such as a warm top and a waterproof.

• mini-tools, for making any emergency repairs.

MTB can be hard work, and you sweat out loads of fluids, so it is important to keep taking little sips of water.

Born in Dijon, France, Anne-Caro, as she is known, is one of the best mountain bikers ever. She has been world downhill champion 12 times, and has won the year-long World Cup four times. Anne-Caro has also won world championships at dual slalom four times, 4X twice, and BMX three times. She won the first-ever BMX Olympic gold medal at the Beijing Olympics in 2008.

ANNE-CAROLINE CHAUSSON

Cross-country riding is the kind of MTB most people first experience. A good cross-country ride usually has a bit of everything: some smooth trails through beautiful countryside, narrow paths through woods and undergrowth, bumpy downhills, and a bit of climbing – some riders *like* going uphill!

Cross-country bikes

The bikes used for cross-country are usually a bit lighter than other mountain bikes. The riders probably will not be doing jumps or hitting big rocks, so the bikes do not have to be as strong as downhill bikes. When riding uphill, though, having less weight in the frame and wheels can make the difference between making it to the top and having to get off and push.

During a race, the first rider to the top of the hill has a nice, clear run at the rest of the course.

Riding out into the countryside with a group of friends is a great way to spend a bit of time at the weekend or during school holidays.

Top guidebooks
- **Mountain Biking Europe (Footprint)** – *a detailed guide to just about every MTB area in Europe. This book is worth picking up for the inspiring photographs alone.*
- **Montana Singletrack (Beartooth Guides)** – *contains some of the best rides in one of the USA's best states for MTB.*

Single track heaven

There is one kind of riding all mountain bikers love – single track. Single track gets it name from the fact that the trails are only wide enough for a single bike at a time to pass along them. Single track can run through all kinds of landscape, from rocky slopes to fields and gorse-covered hillsides.

Many riders prefer single track that goes through woods: swooping through gaps between the trees is like racing in your own personal slalom contest. Hearing your friend's bike clattering along behind just encourages you to pedal that bit harder.

In cross-country racing, the riders pedal around a circuit a set number of times, and the first rider across the finish line wins. The courses range from undemanding, flat routes that can be covered at high speed to tricky technical challenges that demand a lot of bike-handling skill.

Local races

In the past, small, local cross-country races took place most weekends. Today, cross-country racing is less popular. It is sometimes possible to find a local MTB race, but more often riders join in with a cyclo-cross race (see page 6).

Riders test out the course for the cross-country MTB race at the 2012 Olympics.

Olympic racers

Cross-country riding is currently the only way for mountain bikers to get to the Olympics. Cross-country first appeared in the Olympics in 1996, at the Atlanta Games.

Hadleigh Park in Essex is the home of MTB at the London Olympics. The course is different from other Olympic courses because it is on open hillside rather than in a wooded area. Open hillside is exciting for spectators, but it makes racing more difficult because it is harder to get away from pursuers if they can see how far ahead you are.

Even with 30 gears, sometimes you just have to get off and push!

Julien Absalon comes from the Vosges region of France. The area's wooded hills are perfect for cross-country riding. Absalon dominated cross-country racing between 2004 and 2008. He won Olympic gold in Athens (2004) and Beijing (2008), and won the MTB world championship every year from 2004 to 2007.

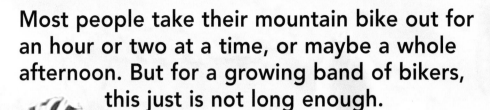

Most people take their mountain bike out for an hour or two at a time, or maybe a whole afternoon. But for a growing band of bikers, this just is not long enough. They like to take in events that last a whole day and night – or even longer.

A congested start to the Cape Epic. Each year, the race is held over eight days. Bikers ride through about 800 kilometres of the unspoilt nature of the Western Cape, South Africa.

24-hour racing

Races lasting 24 hours usually start at midday on a Saturday and finish at midday on Sunday. The riders can compete solo, in pairs or in teams of four. The races have a real party atmosphere, with food stalls, places to buy replacements for broken kit, DJ booths and bike washes. The winners are those who do the most laps, but most riders are there mainly to have a good time.

By night-time in a 24-hour race, riders will be exhausted. The woods can be a spooky place!

Long-distance endurance

For real long-distance riding fans, there are mountain bike races that take days to finish. These are usually solo rides, covering hundreds of kilometres. Sometimes, the racers have to carry all their kit with them in **panniers** or a **trailer**. In most long-distance races, though, a **support team** carries cooking and camping gear, plus spare clothes, leaving the rider free to go as fast as possible.

Three top endurance races
- *Great Divide Race – an annual race down the spine of North America, from Canada to Mexico.*
- *Trans-Wales – a week-long race across Wales, with the riders following specially designed routes each day.*
- *Trans-Rockies – racers ride 600 kilometres across the beautiful Canadian landscape in a week.*

One of the spiritual homes of MTB is the North Shore Mountains of Vancouver, in Canada, an area that is filled with old forests. Here, mosses hang down from the trees and thick undergrowth deadens the sound, making it a magical place to ride.

A ladder ride over marshy ground on the North Shore.

Ladder riders

The wet weather of the North Shore means that in places, boggy soil can swallow a bike up to its wheel **hubs**. Elsewhere, streams have cut deep chasms into the hillsides. To get over these obstacles, riders started building '**ladders**' – raised wooden paths, along which they could ride.

Extreme skills

The demands of ladder riding meant that the riders quickly became experts at bike handling. Every year, they tackled harder and harder routes. Today, North Shore riding includes a huge bag of tricks, including jumps, riding down near-vertical rock faces, and balance skills such as hopping a bike around a 90 degree bend on a ladder 10 metres above the ground.

This purpose-built ladder track offers an extreme challenge to a rider's skills.

Top North Shore videos
You can find tasters of these videos on the North Shore Mountain Biking website (www.nsmb.com):
- *Trials of the Trails – great footage of trail riding, as well as a discussion of the environmental impact of MTB.*
- *Drop In New Zealand – also features dirt jumping and a bit of skate park action, but the trail riding is the highlight.*
- *Kranked 7: The Cackle Factor – great North Shore footage, plus some breath-taking freeriding.*

If you are a fan of snowboarding, you will probably know all about boardercross. It is a thrills-and-spills race between four snowboarders, racing side-by-side down a course of jumps and sharp turns. Four-cross, which is usually written '4X', is a mountain-bike version of the same thing.

Dual slalom and the birth of 4X

Before 4X, there was a similar event called dual slalom. In this, two riders raced down parallel courses, with the first to finish winning. 4X grew out of dual slalom, but instead of racing down four parallel courses, the riders all race down the same one. The course features jumps, banked turns known as **berms**, and other obstacles to test the riders.

One of MTB's key cornering skills is to always look ahead where you want to go, rather than at the ground under your front wheel.

4X contests

Contests start with every rider doing a timed run. The fastest 50 per cent of riders go through to the knockout stages. In these, four riders leave the start gates at the same time. They ride the course side-by-side, with either the first two or just the winner going through to the next round. After each round, the field is reduced by at least half, so the competition is fast and furious. There are always plenty of spectator-pleasing crashes, as racers desperately try to nab one of the top places.

Either this rider is way ahead... or he crashed and is dead last!

Australia's Jared Graves is one of the world's top 4X riders. He won the season-long World Cup competition in 2009 and 2010, and was also world champion in 2009 and 2010. Graves is also a top BMX rider, having come second in the 2008 World Cup and sixth at the 2008 Beijing Olympics. In his spare time, he takes part in top-level downhill races as well.

Most bikers start riding downhill by trying to get down their favourite route just a little bit faster than the last time (and just a little bit faster than their friends). But watch out – the challenge of getting down a slope as fast as you can is **addictive**.

Downhill bikes have to be very strong to absorb big hits!

Heavy metal riders

Downhill racing is the heavy metal of MTB – not everyone likes it, but you cannot ignore it. The top riders are among a tiny number of people who can control a bike at speeds of 100 kph, avoiding roots, rocks and trees as they go. Few riders have reflexes that good, or are able to beat the fear of having a serious accident.

Urban downhill
When you think of MTB, you probably think of the countryside. Some downhill races, though, take place in cities. The riders clatter down steps, cross bridges, jump over roads and career down concrete slopes.

Urban downhills have taken place in (among other cities):
- *Lisbon, Portugal*
- *Sarajevo, Bosnia*
- *Edinburgh, Scotland*
- *Cagliari, Sardinia*
Key 'urban downhill' into YouTube to find clips of the action.

Downhill courses

Most downhill courses combine sections of track where the riders can go full speed with more technical challenges. It is often possible to ride around obstacles, but this is usually slower. This means the most skilled riders are able to set the fastest times.

Downhill racing is real crowd pleaser, as the riders clatter down tricky routes at high speed.

Downhill bikes and kit

Downhill bikes look almost like motocross bikes without engines. Because they travel downhill only, the bikes have to be tough, which makes them heavy. Downhill racers wear full body armour to protect themselves in a crash. A rider's chest, neck, shoulders, elbows, hips and knees are all covered by hard armour. Racers also wear protective gloves, **full-face** helmets and goggles.

There are lots of good things about MTB. Most of all, it is fun and it keeps you fit. There is even evidence that regular exercise can improve your marks at school! MTB can also be dangerous – riders have been badly injured, or even killed, in accidents. So it pays to make your riding as safe as possible.

Top tips for riding safe

Making a few simple checks every time you ride, and following some simple guidelines, can help to make MTB as safe as possible:

- equipment – always wear a helmet, and other safety kit if you are doing extreme riding.

- check your bike before every ride – make sure the wheels are securely attached, the brakes work and the handlebars and saddle are secure.

- know how to fall – if you do come off your bike, relax and try to roll or slide away, instead of slamming into the ground, a tree or a rock.

Riding alone is never a good idea, and when riding in a group make sure everyone sticks together. Always ride at the pace of the slowest person, so that they don't fall behind.

Riding rules
MTB is popular, and sometimes the trails get busy. Riders have developed a few guidelines to make things flow smoothly:
- *try not to stop on a narrow or steep section of trail, where other riders will be forced to stop behind you.*
- *let faster riders past (as soon as there is a safe place to stop) if you can hear them catching up behind.*
- *if you catch someone up, do not shout or harass them – it will make them nervous (and probably slower). Wait for them to let you past.*

- do not push too hard – never be pushed into trying something you are worried about, such as a big jump or a steep downhill. Fear makes your body tense up, which makes it unlikely that you will succeed.

- never follow someone else's **line** – just because there are tyre tracks going along a trail, it does not mean you can follow at full speed. The person in front might be a better rider than you – or they might be wrapped around a tree just around the corner.

Right now, this rider is wondering whether taking part in a race over snow was such a good idea after all.

There are tens of thousands of great places to go riding – wherever there is a bit of countryside, you will find people riding across it on knobbly tyred bikes. But where would you go riding if you won so much money that you could fly anywhere you wanted in a private jet? Here are a few ideas:

Marin County, California, USA

You would have to take a trip to the place where MTB as we know it began – Marin County, and in particular Mount Tamalpais. The area has everything from long downhills to all-day cross-country rides.

Durango, Colorado, USA

Durango is where the first-ever mountain-bike world championships was held. It has just about every kind of riding, from downhills to cross-country trails.

Snowy Mountains, Australia

In winter, you can find some of Australia's best ski runs in the Snowy Mountains, but in summer the area is great for MTB. In particular, the area around Mount Beauty, which is sometimes called Australia's mountain-bike capital, is worth a visit.

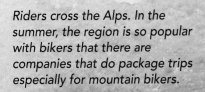

Riders cross the Alps. In the summer, the region is so popular with bikers that there are companies that do package trips especially for mountain bikers.

Chamonix, France

The Chamonix Valley is great for all kinds of extreme sports, especially MTB. Ski lifts carry you and your bike high up into the mountains, and you can spend all day zig-zagging your way down.

Åre, Sweden

Åre (pronounced 'ore-uh') is mostly about **lift-assisted** downhill and freeride trails, and there is not much cross-country riding here.

Afan Forest Park, Wales

Some brilliantly designed trails wind up and down the slopes of this valley. The single track through the forests is really exciting, and the tricky sections of Whytes Level and The Wall challenge even the best riders.

7stanes, Scotland

Not one, but eight MTB areas, showing off the best of Scotland's trails. At one of the areas, Innerleithen, ordinary riders can attempt the challenge of the UK's only World Cup downhill course.

A rider is put through his paces at the Downhill World Cup in Scotland.

addictive

describes something that is hard to stop once you have started.

beach cruisers

old-fashioned American single-speed bikes with big 'balloon' tyres and wide handlebars.

berms

turns that are banked up, or raised, on one side.

dirt jumping

activity shared between mountain bikers and BMXers, where the riders build up dirt ramps to jump off.

full-face

describes a helmet that protects the rider's chin and jaw as well as the head.

freeride MTB

a type of MTB where there is no set course. Riders aim to make their way down the trail on the most creative line possible. Freeriding tests riders' style, control and speed.

hubs

middle part of a wheel, which allows the wheel to spin around.

ladders

raised paths made out of wooden poles and planks, which allow riders to cross boggy ground.

lift-assisted

using a ski lift to go uphill.

line

route or direction riders go along the trail.

panniers

bags for carrying luggage. They are attached to the back of a bike, either side of the rear wheel.

support team

person or group of people who provide a rider with help during a race.

trailer

one- or two-wheeled carrying platform that is towed behind a bike.

trailhead

place where a mountain-bike trail begins.

travel

amount of movement a bike's suspension has, and so how big a shock it can absorb.

Competitions and organizations

The three biggest MTB competitions are the World Cup, the World Championships and the Olympic Games.

The World Cup is a season-long set of competitions, which decides the best rider over the course of the whole year. The World Championships are a one-off event where the world champion is crowned. Both are run by cycling's international governing body, the UCI (*Union Cycliste Internationale*). Go to www.uci.ch and click on 'Mountain bike' for details of the latest events and World Cup rankings.

The Olympic Games are run by the IOC (International Olympic Committee): go to www.olympic.org and click on 'Cycling' then 'Mountain bike' for information about past medalists, equipment and the history of the sport.

Online magazines

www.nsmb.com
Canada-based online magazine of the North Shore Mountain Bike group, with good articles of riders, equipment and news, plus an excellent videos section where you can watch clips of some amazing riding.

www.imbikemag.com
International Mountainbike Magazine carries a range of articles about kit, technique, places to ride and much more.

www.singletrackworld.com
Online wing of a print magazine, this site has a good range of articles, plus a very good forum where you can contact other riders for advice about technique, equipment, places to ride and just about anything else to do with MTB.

These are the lists of contents for each title in Adrenalin Rush:

Snowboarding

Hitting the slopes • The birth of snowboarding • Snowboarding today • Snowboard design • Equipment and clothing • Piste riding • Big air • Boardercross • Riding freestyle • Freeriding fun • Staying alive • Snowboard hotspots • Extreme snowboarding

MTB

Hit the dirt • Pioneers of MTB • MTB conquers the world • Types of bike • Equipment and clothing • Cross-country • Cross-country racing • Long-haul heroes • North Shore style • Four-cross • Downhill racers • Staying alive • Mountain bike hotspots

BMX

One gear is plenty • BMX takes over the world • The rebirth of BMX • Bike love • Equipment and clothing • Street riding • Ramps and vert riding • Flatland skills • Dirt jumping • BMX racing • Racetrack skills • Staying alive • BMX hotspots

Skateboarding

Hitting the concrete • Pioneers of skating • Conquering the world • Board meeting • Equipment and clothing • Street skating • Ramping up • Vert and mega ramps • Flatland tricks • Longboard riding • Going downhill – fast! • Staying alive • Skateboard hotspots